Circle:

There are many faces from many places.

Circle: 2 [EXIT]   2 ☂   4 🧳   1 📰   1 🏸   1 🏌️

There are animals to see for the whole family.

PLEASE! DO NOT FEED THE ANIMALS!

Circle:

Animals play in the park today.

Circle:

Dinosaurs romp in the muddy swamp.

Circle: 1 ⌇ 1 🐟 1 🐦 3 🦟 4 🦋 2 🐊 1 🐦

Animals kick and prance at the country dance.

Circle:

People meet on a small-town street.

Circle:

Look and see part of our history.

Circle: | 🍶 | **2** | 🖌️ | 🖼️ | | **3** | 🧴 | | 🎨

"Let's get more and more at the grocery store!"

Circle:

There are toys galore in your favorite store.

Circle:

Mother does not know which way to go.

Circle:

LOST AND FOUND

TICKET

3

2

A castle land is built from sand.

Circle: 2 👓 2 🥿 3 ⛵ | 🪣 | 🧴 | 📷

There are many things to see from the top of a tree.

People are busy when meeting in the city.

Circle: 4 | | | | | 2

Many signs invite birds to dine.

Circle: | 3 | | | | | | 2 |

"Oh no! Who let the animals go?"

Circle: 2 [gerbil] | 1 [dog] | 2 [bone] | 2 [cat] | 1 [collar] | 1 [parrot]

16

Take a look at the things around Cook.

Circle:

Find birthday surprises and giveaway prizes.

Circle:

Strange things can be found under this ground.

Circle: 3 🦎 2 〰️ 1 🪺 6 🪱 6 🐛 1 🦎

Outer space can be a fun place.

Circle: | | | 2 | | |

It's time to get away on a hot summer day.

"I serve afternoon tea to Kitty and me."

Circle: 6 🍀 | 🐛 | 4 🐝 | 🏒 | 5 🌷 | 🐦 | 🧤🧤

The elves work hard in their tiny yard.

Circle:

24

In this classroom of clowns, many things can be found.

Circle:

25

Mother is bossing at the turtle crossing.

Circle:
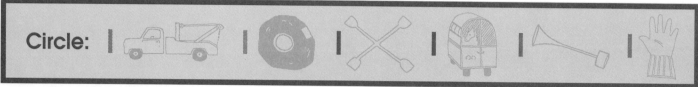

Fido and friends are near the end.

Circle:

A mermaid is asleep in the ocean deep.

Circle: 3 1 4 2 1

Many things are strewn around this boy's room.

Circle:

The barn is the setting for a scarecrow wedding.

Circle:

We reap good food to eat.

Circle: **3**  **2**   **1**   **5**   **4**   **1**

Fun with Jester makes dinner better.

Circle: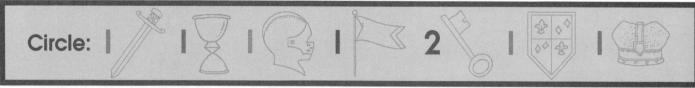